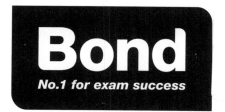

Bond
No.1 for exam success

English and **Verbal Reasoning**

10 Minute Tests

CEM
(Durham University)

9–10 years

OXFORD
UNIVERSITY PRESS

Test 1: **Comprehension**

Read the text carefully and answer the questions that follow.

Taroudant

The searing sun burned so brightly. Fatima looked on as two Berber
women were herding goats and sheep onto a dirt path that snaked up the
mountainside. The goats would climb the trees to feast on the argan fruit
during the cooler weather, but now that it was summertime, the temperature
had increased, shrivelling up everything green. There would be some sweet,   5
grassy pastureland higher up the mountain.

Fatima could not wait to reach home. The path underfoot was too hot, leaving
the soles of her feet on fire and even with her sunglasses on, the merciless
sun found a route to burn her eyes. She crossed over the noisy road, dodging
vehicles that swerved left and then right, and made her way to a busy stall.   10
She could never resist the sweet, sticky dates that were clumped together like
pyramids: some rolled in crushed almonds, others stuffed with sultanas and
honey. Fatima then bought four fat oranges and some lemons before heading
home and away from the bustle and noise.

She crossed the road and turned down a narrow pathway, then turned left   15
and left again. Within a minute, the doorway to her home was unlocked, and
she let herself in. Fatima kicked off her shoes and rejoiced as the cold, tiled
floor soothed her feet. She placed the bulging bag of fruit on the table, which
overlooked a small fountain in the centre of the courtyard. Fatima selected
a plump date and chewed it thoughtfully. The fragrant smells of rosemary,   20
lavender and roses scented the air, which felt fresh. Fatima breathed deeply
and happily as she settled into her chair. The bustle and noise of the day was
soon replaced with the sound of trickling water and a serene calmness. Fatima
closed her eyes.

1   Where were the women herding the goats and sheep?

_____

2   How did the goats feed when the weather was less hot?

_____

_____

3 Give **THREE** ways that Fatima felt different at the end of the text compared to at the beginning of the text.

_____

_____

_____

4 The text says, 'Fatima could not wait to get home.' Why do you think she did not go directly home?

_____

What do these words mean as used in the text?

5 searing (line 1) _____

6 merciless (line 8) _____

7 bustle (line 14) _____

8 bulging (line 18) _____

Use a line to match each literary device to the example from the text.

9 simile   leaving the soles of her feet on fire

10 metaphor   the merciless sun

11 personification   dates that were clumped together like pyramids

Test 2: **Missing Words**

Read the following text and add one word from the list to each space so that the text makes sense. There are more words than there are spaces so some will be left out, but each word can only be used once.

brave	~~clattered~~	~~gripped~~	horror
~~manically~~	silhouette	perplexed	~~surely~~
throbbed	~~tugged~~	~~unwise~~	victim

1–6 The outline of the monster was clear to see. It raised its fierce arms and waved

them _____manically_____ ✓ around its head. Austin swallowed hard. The

monster may well kill him, but he would at least make it known that he was brave,

even if he didn't feel it. Austin forced every part of his body to tighten up as he

_____gripped_____ ✓ the curtain with both hands. Without losing his

nerve, Austin closed his eyes tight, and then with all of his strength he sharply

_____tugged_____ ✓ the curtain to the right.

The heavy metal rings _____clattered_____ ✓ across the steel pole with a

deafening roar as Austin forced his eyes open to see the terrifying monster. The

winter wind blew the bare branches of the hawthorn tree, the sharp twigs stretched

out over the pathway. Austin frowned as he stood _____Surely_____ ✗ .

He felt that perhaps it would be _____unwise_____ ✓ to tell his friends at

school how scared he had been … of a tree!

Find the three-letter word that is needed to complete each word so that each sentence makes sense. The missing three letters must make a word.

Example: The boy pedalled his b____*icy*____cle up the hill. (bicycle)

7   Abathnut counted the number of books he w____*ant*____ed to borrow. ✓

8   The tortoise yawned as she sun____*bath*____hed in the July afternoon. ✓

9   The beehives were full of h____*one*____y in the summer. ✓

10 The dog was c____~~ett~~____ing the neighbour's cat. ✓
        has

The following sentences all have **ONE** word missing. Complete the sentences by selecting a word from options **a–e**.

11 The ___(e)___ *museum* had many Egyptian and Middle Eastern artefacts. ✓

    a church   **b** hotel   **c** manor   **d** planetarium   **(e)** museum

12 Bob was so ____*relieved*____ when he found his passport. ✓

    a angry   **b** pacified   **(c)** relieved   **d** threatened   **e** irritated

13 There were many apple, pear and plum trees in the ___(e) *forest*___. ✗

    a farm   **b** house   **c** orchard   **d** dell   **(e)** forest

14 Susan and Paul always travelled first class by ___(d) *plane*___. ✓

    a car   **b** yacht   **c** taxi   **(d)** plane   **e** coach

15 The theatre ___~~that~~ (d) *audience*___ was excited to see the new play. ✓

    a congregation   **b** pupils   **c** customers   **(d)** audience   **e** clients

13/15 ✓

Test 3: **Matching Words**

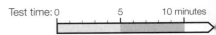

Select the **ONE** word on the right that has the most **SIMILAR** meaning to the word on the left. Underline the correct answer.

1   persuade   **a** motivate   **b** discourage   **c** cocoon   **d** deter   **e** play

2   interrupt   **a** assist   **b** disturb   **c** help   **d** speech   **e** middle

3   rhythm   **a** drum   **b** bass   **c** drone   **d** beat   **e** perform

4   swell   **a** decrease   **b** increase   **c** few   **d** several   **e** offend

5   achieve   **a** find   **b** fail   **c** aim   **d** accuse   **e** accomplish

6   familiar   **a** unsure   **b** allocated   **c** again   **d** unknown   **e** recognised

Select the **ONE** word on the right that has the most **OPPOSITE** meaning to the word on the left. Underline the correct answer.

7   build   **a** end   **b** create   **c** destroy   **d** manage   **e** try

8   modern   **a** contemporary   **b** soon   **c** lost   **d** historic   **e** now

9   separate   **a** split   **b** observe   **c** divide   **d** untie   **e** unite

10   surprise   **a** predict   **b** assume   **c** party   **d** expected   **e** stun

11   considered   **a** thought   **b** kind   **c** mean   **d** rash   **e** reign

12   accidental   **a** sorry   **b** guarded   **c** regular   **d** deliberate   **e** disordered

Read the following sentences and answer the questions with the most sensible word.

'Toby condensed his story so that it would fit onto one page.'

13 What does the word 'condensed' mean as used in the sentence?

   a created   **b** wrote   **c** adapted   **d** lengthened   **(e)** shortened ✓

'Mandy constructed a new shed to replace the old one.'

14 What does the word 'constructed' mean as used in the sentence?

   a brought   **b** bought   **(c)** built   **d** fixed   **e** framed ✓

'Sian could not believe the rudeness of the man who barged past.'

15 What does the word 'barged' mean as used in the sentence?

   a smiled   **b** stared   **(c)** charged   **d** sailed   **e** boated ✓

'Noah looked at his watch anxiously as he still had homework to complete.'

16 What does the word 'anxiously' mean as used in the sentence?

   (a) nervously   **b** viciously   **c** fiercely   **d** slowly   **e** comprehensively ✓

'Rose had a career that meant she travelled throughout Europe.'

17 What does the word 'career' mean as used in the sentence?

   a holiday   **b** vacation   **(c)** hobby   **(d)** occupation   **e** oration ✗

'The benevolent old sailor gave all of his wages to the hospice.'

18 What does the word 'benevolent' mean as used in the sentence?

   a mean   **b** wealthy   **c** poor   **d** hostile   **(e)** kind ✓

Test 4: **Mixed**

Read the text carefully and answer the questions that follow.

Molly's Best Decision

Molly had always wanted to be a mechanical engineer like her father and
grandfather, so it was surprising when she suddenly changed her mind.
Molly didn't want to let her family down, but the first year at university had
clarified her thoughts. Molly wanted to be a chemical engineer and now,
years later, here she was in the laboratory working hard to lead her team.   5
She oversaw sample collections and specimen testing, through to all phases
of clinical research. Molly checked trial data every day and was painstaking
in her approach. Today was the most important day of her life. After years of
working on this specific project, the results were beyond exciting. The press
photographers clicked away on their cameras while journalists asked so many   10
questions. Molly smiled broadly. "Yes," she replied. "Yes, I can confirm that we
do now have a cure."

1   What job did Molly originally want? Underline the correct answer.

   a   a journalist

   b   a press photographer

   c   a chemical engineer

   d   an electrical engineer

   e   a mechanical engineer

2   Select the **TWO** false statements. Underline the correct answers.

   a   Molly's job was involved in research.

   b   Molly worked in a laboratory.

   c   Molly followed in her father's footsteps.

   d   Molly studied at university.

   e   Molly was carefree and careless in her approach to work.

3 Why did Molly smile broadly? Underline the **ONE** correct answer.

1

   a   Molly loved journalists.

   b   Molly wanted to look friendly in the press photographs.

   c   Molly had some exciting, happy news to share.

   d   Molly enjoyed her job every day.

   e   Molly was relieved that the project was finally over.

Find the three-letter word that is needed to complete each word so that each sentence makes sense. The missing three letters must make a word.

4

4 We had a wedding p_____ographer who was there all day.

5 The housing association rented out lots of proper_____s.

6 The chef had baked a _____derful meal for us.

7 The gar_____ centre had some lovely plants on sale.

Select the **ONE** word on the right that has the most **SIMILAR** meaning to the word on the left. Underline the correct answer.

5

8 outlook   **a** view   **b** spectate   **c** glass   **d** object   **e** reject

9 pause   **a** go   **b** cancel   **c** rest   **d** eject   **e** feet

10 sag   **a** taut   **b** tighten   **c** plump   **d** droop   **e** fall

11 latest   **a** delayed   **b** tardy   **c** newest   **d** oldest   **e** longest

12 hunt   **a** search   **b** find   **c** locate   **d** study   **e** concentrate

Total   13

Test 5: **Missing Letters**

Find the three-letter word that is needed to complete each word so that each sentence makes sense. The missing three letters must make a word. Underline the **TWO** answers needed from options **a–e**.

Example: I am just pop_pin_g to the shop to buy some fur_nit_ure polish.

 a pan **b** <u>pin</u> **c** pun **d** net **e** <u>nit</u>

1 There were some attr_act_ive pictures on the cal_end_ar.

 a ace **(b)** act **c** art **(d)** end **e** ere

2 Solomon's new h_air_style was very f_ash_ionable.

 a act **(b)** air **c** are **(d)** ash **e** ate

3 Ellie put some _she_lving up to store her orna_men_ts.

 a bat **b** man **(c)** men **(d)** she **e** shy

4 The train hurt_led_ past the little snow-covered vil_lag_es en route to the mountains.

 a lad **(b)** lag **c** lap **(d)** led **e** leg

Find the missing four letters that need to be added to these words so that the sentence makes sense. The four letters do not have to make a word.

Example: I have great r_____m so I love to dance.

 a ithe **b** itit **c** <u>hyth</u> **d** hith **e** itth

5 The woman who reported the crime was a valuable wi_tnes_s.

 a nner **b** nter **(c)** tnes **d** tnis **e** ntar

6 Six of the cousins sat to_geth_er giggling at the party.

 a gath **(b)** geth **c** gith **d** goth **e** guth

7 Alt _houg_ h we were excited, we tried to keep as calm as possible.

   a oget   **b** thou   **c** houg   **d** ougg   **e** hoog

8 There was a subs _tant_ ial fall of snow during the night.

   a dand   **b** tand   **c** tant   **d** tend   **e** tent

Find the missing four letters that need to be added to the letters in capitals to make a new word. The new word will complete the sentence sensibly. The four letters do not have to make a word.

5

Example: I BHT a basket of tasty food to the picnic. (brought)

   a OURT   **b** ROUG   **c** MIGH   **d** TRUT   **e** LOUH

9 Zidan borrowed some books from the school LRY. *library*

   a EERY   **b** IRRY   **c** IARY   **d** IBRA   **e** IERY

10 We baked some POES to serve at the party. *Potatoes*

   a OAOW   **b** OTAT   **c** EAOE   **d** AAOE   **e** OAOU

11 The customers were COMNING because the shop was not open. *Complaining*

   a PLAI   **b** PLAY   **c** OPEN   **d** OPEA   **e** OBAI

12 The majestic waterfalls CDED down the sides of the mountains.

   a ASCA   **b** SCAD   **c** ASSA   **d** ASKA   **e** ASCE

13 Although the wards were not full, the nurses were still EXELY busy.

   a TRIM   **b** REML   **c** TEEM   **d** TEAY   **e** TREM

Test 6: **Missing Words**

Choose **ONE** word that is the best fit in each of these sentences. Underline your answer from options **a–d**.

1 The tailor had some beautiful tweed _____ from which to make a suit.

   a roll   **b** construction   **c** wood   **d** material

2 We worked really hard at the restaurant as we were so _____.

   a quiet   **b** slack   **c** busy   **d** bossy

3 The charity held an _____ fundraising evening each summer.

   a yearly   **b** annual   **c** end   **d** old

4 After supper he would _____ into his shed for an hour or two.

   a study   **b** work   **c** appear   **d** disappear

5 Between 1577 and 1580, Francis Drake _____ the world on his ship.

   a cruised   **b** rode   **c** circumnavigated   **d** ringing

---

In each of the following sentences, there is a short phrase missing. Complete each sentence by selecting one short phrase from options **a–e** that is the best fit. Underline your answer.

6 Mrs Zhang worked hard _____ her grandchildren.

   a looking out   **b** looking after   **c** looking for   **d** looking in   **e** looking over

7 She also helped out in the family business and _____ extremely house-proud.

   a she is   **b** she has   **c** she was   **d** she am   **e** she were

8 What she really enjoyed doing though _____ at the night sky from an observatory she had created in her garden shed.

a were looking **b** were looked **c** were look **d** was looking **e** was looked

9 The night sky is like a vast black blanket filled _____ of stars.

a with clusters **b** with bunches **c** with flocks **d** with herds **e** with gaggles

10 Sometimes _____ possible to see shooting stars that fly across the universe.

a it am **b** that is **c** which is **d** it is **e** it are

---

Find the three-letter word that is needed to complete each word so that each sentence makes sense. The missing three letters must make a word. Underline your answer from options **a–e**.

5

Example: The boy pedalled his b_____cle up the hill.

a act **b** _icy_ **c** lay **d** air **e** ice

11 The Queen's main resi_____ce is at Buckingham Palace.
a dan **b** den **c** din **d** don **e** dun

12 The store ma_____er of the toy shop decided to hold an autumn sale.

a nag **b** gag **c** sag **d** tag **e** wag

13 Auntie Shirley lit eleven c_____les on my birthday cake.

a ace **b** and **c** art **d** kin **e** kit

14 The tired boy put on his py_____as before climbing into bed.

a dam **b** gem **c** gum **d** jam **e** jar

15 Our orchestra reh_____sed all weekend to prepare for the concert.

a are **b** ear **c** err **d** her **e** ire

Total | 15

Test 7: **Matching Words**

Look at the words in the grid and then use them to answer the questions that follow.

a depart	**b** extreme	**c** ought	**d** retain	**e** legendary
f launder	**g** pause	**h** washing	**i** ordinary	**j** wander
k wonder	**l** cleanse	**m** appear	**n** wash	**o** go
p magical	**q** idea	**r** purify	**s** famous	**t** turn
u normal	**v** wonderful	**w** halt	**x** rotate	**y** thought

1 Find **TWO** words that are **OPPOSITE** to the word 'special'.

_____   _____

2 Find **TWO** words that are **OPPOSITE** to the word 'arrive'.

_____   _____

3 Find **TWO** words that are most **SIMILAR** to the word 'stop'.

_____   _____

4 Find **TWO** words that are most **SIMILAR** to the word 'known'.

_____   _____

5 Find **TWO** words that are most **SIMILAR** to the word 'spin'.

_____   _____

Read the following sentences and answer the questions with the most sensible word.

'The tournament was held between six teams.'

6 What does the word 'tournament' mean as used in the sentence?
   a committee   **b** object   **c** journey   **d** tour   **e** competition

'Norm said that his favourite beverage was coffee, but Artem preferred tea.'

7 What does the word 'beverage' mean as used in the sentence?

    a snack   **b** food   **c** drink   **d** refresher   **e** feast

'The temperature on the thermometer proved he was unwell.'

8 What does the word 'proved' mean as used in the sentence?

    a presumed   **b** assumed   **c** told   **d** raised   **e** confirmed

'Yuwei couldn't recollect the last time she had an incorrect spelling.'

9 What does the word 'recollect' mean as used in the sentence?

    a remember   **b** reason   **c** show   **d** forget   **e** recognise

'The gales were so severe that several trees were uprooted.'

10 What does the word 'severe' mean as used in the sentence?

    a wet   **b** weak   **c** authoritative   **d** gentle   **e** intense

---

Select the **ONE** word on the right that has the most **SIMILAR** meaning to the word on the left. Underline the correct answer.

5

11 develop   **a** photograph   **b** purge   **c** progress   **d** purify   **e** passage

12 variety   **a** assortment   **b** similar   **c** tangle   **d** territory   **e** meander

13 necessary   **a** needing   **b** wanting   **c** giving   **d** needed   **e** needy

14 occur   **a** sweet   **b** magical   **c** happen   **d** return   **e** twist

15 stoop   **a** fall   **b** old   **c** bend   **d** plait   **e** halt

Total   20

Test 8: **Mixed**

Find the three-letter word that is needed to complete each word so that each sentence makes sense. The missing three letters must make a word. Underline the **TWO** answers needed from options **a–e**.

1   It became app_____nt that Year 6 needed more help with their g_____mar.

    a aim   **b** are   **c** ate   **d** ram   **e** rum

2   Wait before getting so_____hing until you know how much you

    re_____y want it.

    a aim   **b** all   **c** mat   **d** met   **e** rut

3   The King's s_____iers prepa_____ for battle.

    a air   **b** all   **c** old   **d** red   **e** rod

4   Wilma buttoned up her car_____an and straigh_____ed her tie.

    a dad   **b** dig   **c** dog   **d** tan   **e** ten

Choose **ONE** word that is the best fit in each of these sentences. Underline your answer from options **a–d**.

5   We looked up the spelling of our word in a _____.

    a paper   **b** encyclopaedia   **c** book   **d** dictionary

6   We put _____ candles on the cake for Dad's birthday.

    a some   **b** less   **c** least   **d** fewer

7   The storm was awful, with non-stop thunder and _____.

    a lightening   **b** snow   **c** fog   **d** lightning

8 Henry VIII is _____ for his many wives.

    a good   **b** notorious   **c** preferred   **d** grateful

---

Find the missing three letters that complete these words. The three letters do not have to make a word. The same three letters are used for both words.

        5

9 q_____ k e n   q_____ k l y

10 p a s_____ e   _____ n i p s

11 t e l_____ s i o n   r_____ s i o n

12 s p_____ l e   r e m_____ a b l e

13 p u_____ e s   s i_____ i n g

Select the **ONE** word on the right that has the most **SIMILAR** meaning to the word on the left. Underline the correct answer.

        3

14 floppy   **a** drooping   **b** furry   **c** rigid   **d** minute   **e** vast

15 sympathise   **a** cheer   **b** party   **c** argue   **d** explain   **e** commiserate

16 integrate   **a** incorporate   **b** subject   **c** object   **d** parallel   **e** interrupt

Test 9: **Comprehension**

Read the text carefully and then answer the questions that follow.

A Dancing Bear

Gabriel shook the bright yellow tin, rattling the few coins that were in there.
It was hectic as the sales were on, but nobody stopped for him. It wasn't
the best time for collecting. It was bitterly cold so he was glad, for the first
time ever, that he was dressed up like a giant yellow teddy bear. He usually
overheated in the costume. That said, the wind still blew through the fabric, so   **5**
he began to stamp his feet on the cold concrete paving slabs and to swing his
arms around his body to generate a little more heat.

"Look, Mummy, a dancing bear!" a little girl shouted out as she clapped her
hands together in delight. Gabriel looked in horror as the little girl dragged her
mother in front of him. He couldn't let down a little girl, but Gabriel had never   **10**
danced in his life. He continued to kick out his legs, stamp his feet and swing
his arms around as he frantically thought about dance moves, but the more he
moved, the bigger the crowd that gathered. Gabriel knew that nobody would
recognise him dressed as a bear, so he decided to really go for it. He attempted
a moonwalk, he tried a jive, he performed a Scooby Doo; he excelled at the   **15**
cha-cha-cha and the Macarena. He hipped and he hopped, he popped and he
bopped; he had a go at krumping, at breaking and at shaking. He improvised line
dancing and quickstep prancing, he even tried Gangnam Style and he shook his
little bottom until his teddy bear head nearly fell off.

Gabriel handed in the tin that night to the charity coordinator. He had raised so   **20**
much money and yet he had never, ever, EVER had so much fun. Gabriel was
a dancer.

1   What was Gabriel doing in town? Underline **ONE** answer.

    a   He was shopping in the sales.

    b   He had gone there to dance.

    c   He was collecting money for charity.

    d   He was dressing up.

    e   He was meeting someone.

2 Why did Gabriel first begin to dance? Underline **ONE** answer.

⊂ 1

   a   He didn't want to let the little girl down.

   b   He wanted to attract a crowd.

   c   He wanted attention.

   d   He wanted to try out some new dance moves.

   e   He wanted to raise more money.

3 How do you think Gabriel felt when the girl clapped her hands? Underline **ONE** answer.

⊂ 1

   a   He felt pleased that she loved teddy bears.

   b   He felt grateful that it was so cold but in his costume he was warm.

   c   He felt embarrassed as he didn't want anyone to look at him.

   d   He felt scared that the little girl might laugh at him.

   e   He felt thrilled that his dancing was keeping her entertained.

Underline **ONE** word on the right that is closest in meaning to the word on the left, as it is used in the text.

⊂ 4

4 hectic (line 2)   **a** boring   **b** busy   **c** quiet   **d** hot   **e** sleepy

5 generate (line 7)   **a** spend   **b** find   **c** produce   **d** prepare   **e** lose

6 excelled (line 15)   **a** failed   **b** enjoyed   **c** disliked   **d** tried   **e** triumphed

7 attempted (line 14)   **a** liked   **b** felt   **c** persuaded   **d** wanted   **e** tried

Total   7

Test 10: **Missing Words**

Read the following paragraph and add one word from the list to each space so that the paragraph makes sense. There are more words than there are spaces so some will be left out, but each word can only be used once.

chaos	convinced	excited	expressions	gaggle
holiday	happy	honking	impatience	peering
queue	realised	smiling	waddled	

1–10   Jethro was bored. His mum and dad had told him to stay in bed if he woke

up early, but whatever he did, he must stay in his bedroom. Jethro was on

_____ and he was excited. He tiptoed into the lounge and

opened the curtains, only to find a huge _____ of Egyptian

geese waiting to be fed. _____ through the patio door, they

looked at him with _____. Jethro took the loaf of bread that

Mum had put on the kitchen worktop. He didn't want to disappoint the birds, so he

opened the patio doors and began throwing chunks of bread onto the ground. The

geese were soon joined by ducks and drakes who _____

quickly to the front of the queue. Some black swans soon came along and as he

was feeding them, Jethro noticed that the geese were now in the lounge. Jethro

frowned. He wasn't _____ that Mum and Dad would be

happy with so many birds inside the log cabin. Jethro didn't have long to find out

as the _____ geese soon brought Mum and Dad rushing in

from their bedroom. The lounge was in _____. There were

geese on the sofa and ducks on the floor; there were black swans on the worktop and mucky footprints, little feathers, spilt breadcrumbs and all manner of mess and dirt all over the lounge. Jethro looked at his parents' _____ and _____ that he probably shouldn't have left his bedroom.

Find the three-letter word that is needed to complete each word so that each sentence makes sense. The missing three letters must make a word.

Example: The boy pedalled his b___*icy*___cle up the hill. (bicycle)

11 We investig_____d plants in our science lesson today.

12 The baby had a high tempe_____ure, but he is better now.

13 Mum and Dad put up a new _____drobe in my bedroom.

14 We walked around the castle ruins on ho_____ay.

The following sentences all have **ONE** word missing. Complete the sentences by selecting a word from options **a–e**.

15 Josef painted the newly _____ shed before he used it.

    a brought   **b** constructed   **c** paid   **d** wooden   **e** garden

16 Rufus was so happy that there was freshly fallen _____ to play in.

    a wind   **b** thunder   **c** fog   **d** snow   **e** mist

17 On Monday the whole class went on a school _____ to the farm.

    a event   **b** fall   **c** interest   **d** family   **e** visit

4

3

Total 17

Test 11: **Missing Letters**

Add the missing letters to the word on the right to make a word with an **OPPOSITE** meaning to the word on the left.

Example: start   f _i_ n _i_ s _h_   (finish)

1   answer   __ u __ s __ i __ n

2   vertical   h __ r __ z __ n __ a __

3   wonderful   __ r __ a __ f __ l

4   strict   l __ n __ e __ t

5   tolerant   __ r __ j __ d __ c __ d

6   calm   b o i __ t __ r __ u s

Find the missing four letters that need to be added to these words so that the text makes sense. The four letters do not have to make a word.

7–14   Alisha queued for ages with her dad and little sister. Every step closer seemed more

and more ex_____ng. At last they reached the desk and Dad bought

three tickets for the first showing. Alisha then stood in the ref_____ment

area, bedazzled by the huge array of sweets. She began cautiously with some fruit

sweets and chews before she grew in conf_____ce and began to fill her

cup with anything that caught her eye. Next to the sweets there were huge popcorn

mac_____s filled high with sweet and salty golden nuggets. The drinks machines came next and ev_____ally, the family made their way

to screen 10.

Finding their seats in the gloomy da_____ss, Alisha settled herself,

helping her little sister to take off her coat and gloves. With immense excitement,

Alisha sat back like a queen on her t_____e as the curtains

op_____ and the film began.

Find the missing three letters that complete these words. The three letters do not have
to make a word.

8

15 b e _____ i f u l

16 h u r r _____ l y

17 n e g l e _____ d

18 o r c h e _____ a

19 b e g i _____ n g

20 t e c h n _____ g y

21 t r e m e _____ u s

22 f r a _____ c a l l y

23

Test 12: **Mixed**

Read the text carefully and answer the questions that follow.

First Aid Saves Lives

Knowing what to do in an emergency can make the difference between life
and death. Over 17 000 people die every year from accidents and thousands
of these lives could have been saved if first aid had been applied. Dr Preston,
a leading accident doctor, says, "First aid is easy enough for anyone to learn
and can literally save lives."   5

One of the most important aspects of first aid
is to place someone who is unconscious
into the recovery position. To do
this you need to kneel in front of
the unconscious person. First,
place the person's arm at a right   10
angle to their body with the palm
facing upwards. Now take the
person's other arm and lay it
across their chest with the back of their hand against the side of their face.   15
Next, lift their knee and pull it up until their foot is flat on the floor. Finally, pull
the bent knee towards you until they are lying sideways. Always check that
their mouth is clear so that they can breathe.

This small act just might save someone's life until the emergency services
can take over. Why not ask your school to run a first aid course so that you   20
can learn more techniques and skills?

**A person lying in the
recovery position**

1   Why does the text teach you how to put someone in the recovery position?

_____

_____

2   Give **THREE** ways in which you can tell that this is a factual text.

_____

_____

_____

3 Why should you always check someone's mouth?

_____

_____

Find the three-letter word that is needed to complete each word so that each sentence makes sense. The missing three letters must make a word. Underline the **TWO** words from options **a–e**.

12

4 The quiet night was _____ceful and st_____.

   a ail   **b** ill   **c** pea   **d** pop   **e** sty

5 A _____otic limb can be used when it would be treac_____ous to use a person.

   a her   **b** him   **c** his   **d** rob   **e** rod

6 The singer t_____ted that the band had writ_____ a new album.

   a tee   **b** ten   **c** two   **d** wee   **e** wet

7 There was a huge au_____nce at the cinema for the l_____st film release.

   a ate   **b** eat   **c** die   **d** dye   **e** tea

8 We s_____t the afternoon creating home_____e decorations.

   a mad   **b** mid   **c** mud   **d** pan   **e** pen

9 We were able to fly from our reg_____al airport when we began our j_____ney to Portugal.

   a eon   **b** err   **c** ion   **d** our   **e** out

Test 13: **Comprehension**

Read the text carefully and answer the questions that follow.

Origami

The boy was about twelve or thirteen. His appearance had nothing of note and he was instantly forgettable. In fact, nobody realised that he was the entertainment until the dramatic music began. The boy picked up a piece of square white paper and showed it to the audience. They watched him suspiciously until they fell under his spell as he worked the paper, turning it this way and that, folding it here, creasing it there; opening, turning, folding, pleating, reversing. At last he placed the paper down on the table. He had created an exquisite hummingbird.
5

As he forgot the audience, so he held them ever more captive as silver foil paper, patterned paper and silk paper were all transformed under his capable hands and birds, flowers, animals and boxes appeared. With a sudden bow to the audience, the boy broke the enchantment. The audience took just a moment to realise that the show was over before they clapped and applauded wildly. They stood up to give a standing ovation to the young boy, amazed that sheets of paper had kept them mesmerized for over an hour.
10

1 Why did the audience view the boy with suspicion? Underline the correct answer.

a He didn't look like the entertainment.

b They were expecting something different.

c They didn't know what he was going to do with a piece of paper.

d All of the above reasons.

e None of the above reasons.

2 How did the audience react during the performance? Underline the correct answer.

a They were bored.

b They were bewitched.

c They were annoyed.

d They were amused.

e They were frightened.

3 In the first paragraph, the word 'crease' has been written as 'creasing'. Which other word in the same paragraph uses the same spelling rule?

1

   a   folding

   b   turning

   c   pleating

   d   reversing

   e   opening

4 How could the boy best be described? Underline the correct answer.

1

   a   nondescript, artistic, wearisome

   b   colourful, wearisome, hypnotic

   c   nervous, hypnotic, nonchalant

   d   hypnotic, artistic, nondescript

   e   nonchalant, nervous, colourful

Underline **ONE** word on the right that is closest in meaning to the word on the left, as it is used in the text.

5

5 exquisite (line 7)   **a** colourful   **b** beautiful   **c** realistic   **d** weak   **e** fragile

6 transformed (line 9)   **a** moved   **b** created   **c** changed   **d** cut   **e** prior

7 wildly (line 13)   **a** enthusiastically   **b** deftly   **c** quietly   **d** quickly   **e** funnily

8 capable (line 9)   **a** okay   **b** aptitude   **c** talented   **d** suitable   **e** possible

9 mesmerized (line 14)   **a** captivated   **b** rigid   **c** scared   **d** appeared   **e** sleepy

Total 9

Test 14: **Matching Words**

Select the **ONE** word on the right that has the most **SIMILAR** meaning to the word on the left. Underline the correct answer.

1   mimic   **a** impersonate   **b** laugh   **c** silent   **d** free   **e** scare

2   seize   **a** particle   **b** partial   **c** snatch   **d** slip   **e** scarcity

3   derelict   **a** neglected   **b** taste   **c** deserve   **d** need   **e** unclean

4   assemble   **a** gather   **b** spread   **c** temper   **d** shake   **e** deform

5   barrel   **a** cyclic   **b** tunnel   **c** keg   **d** hutch   **e** glass

6   range   **a** running   **b** decorate   **c** frail   **d** set   **e** orangery

---

Read the following sentences and answer the questions with the most sensible word.

'The story needed editing before it could be entered into the competition.'

7   What does the word 'editing' mean as used in the sentence?
    a reading   **b** creating   **c** writing   **d** typing   **e** amending

8   What does the word 'competition' mean as used in the sentence?
    a context   **b** contest   **c** convince   **d** convict   **e** consider

'The king was defeated in battle, but his successor was his son.'

9   What does the word 'defeated' mean as used in the sentence?
    a jubilant   **b** victorious   **c** beaten   **d** ignored   **e** fought

10 What does the word 'successor' mean as used in the sentence?
    a heir   **b** fanatic   **c** child   **d** foe   **e** supporter

'The song had a pretty melody and a steady rhythm.'

11 What does the word 'melody' mean as used in the sentence?

    a voice   **b** instrument   **c** tune   **d** accompaniment   **e** solo

12 What does the word 'steady' mean as used in the sentence?

    a varied   **b** unchanging   **c** ranging   **d** wide   **e** unbalanced

'The dog looked at the roasted meat before grabbing it, unable to resist the temptation.'

13 What does the word 'resist' mean?

    a eat   **b** chase   **c** fight   **d** help   **e** insist

14 What does the word 'temptation' mean?

    a attraction   **b** fear   **c** linger   **d** rove   **e** range

Select the **TWO** odd words out on each line. Select your answers by underlining **TWO** of the options **a–e**.

    6

Example: a friend   **b** companion   **c** compact   **d** converted   **e** buddy

15 **a** rotate   **b** roast   **c** revolve   **d** bake   **e** spin

16 **a** early   **b** late   **c** tardy   **d** punctual   **e** delayed

17 **a** lavish   **b** grasping   **c** plentiful   **d** generous   **e** greedy

18 **a** amusing   **b** entertaining   **c** tiresome   **d** funny   **e** tedious

19 **a** tassel   **b** strand   **c** thread   **d** fringe   **e** cord

20 **a** property   **b** possessions   **c** accurately   **d** correctly   **e** properly

Total   20

Test 15: **Missing Words**

These sentences have been jumbled up and all have **ONE** extra word. Underline the word that is not needed.

Example: so cream <u>eat</u> the were cakes delicious

           (The cream cakes were so delicious.)

1   dog for new aquarium bought we a kennel our

2   show mechanic wonderful put on the a studio dance

3   cakes had our sauce with vegetable we pasta

4   the wind rain street was the so heavy the flooded that water

5   a after before breath deep he swimming took underwater

6   street the base corner the stood house the on of

The following sentences all have **ONE** word missing. Complete the sentences by selecting a word from options **a–e**.

7   We travelled to Lima, the _____ of Peru in South America.

    a county   **b** country   **c** capital   **d** continent   **e** canton

8   The number twenty-five is a _____ number.

    a cube   **b** square   **c** prime   **d** triangular   **e** even

9   The mountain gorillas were the _____ of the zoo.

    a highlight   **b** lowlight   **c** light   **d** firelight   **e** lamplight

10 As the sun sank below the _____, the sky was bathed in fiery red and orange.

    a stars   **b** moon   **c** diagonal   **d** horizon   **e** vertices

11 They _____ the tiny boat through the dangerous sandbanks.

    a run   **b** flew   **c** steeled   **d** stole   **e** steered

12 The band recorded their third album which they _____ would do well.

    a knowing   **b** think   **c** hopped   **d** hooped   **e** hoped

---

Read the following paragraph and add one word from the list to each space so that the paragraph makes sense. There are more words than there are spaces, so some will be left out, but each word can only be used once.

    6

    bears   berries   exports   gains   plump   producer   ripe   stripped

–18 The tall Arabica coffee tree _____ a great many

little red coffee _____. The heavy rain makes the

berries _____, while the warm sun makes them

_____. After the outer skin and pulp are removed, the

seed inside is ready to use. The coffee seeds are called 'beans' because they

look like beans. South America is the source of nearly half of the world's coffee

_____ and Brazil is the largest _____.

Test 16: **Mixed**

Read the text carefully and answer the questions that follow.

Madeline Syers

The 1908 Summer Olympic Games were going to be held in Rome. Sadly, the volcano Vesuvius erupted in 1906 and because of this, the Olympics were hosted by London instead. Twenty-two countries participated in twenty-two sports from aquatics and archery to tug-of-war and wrestling.

In figure skating, England had Florence Madeline Syers – known as Madge –   **5**
as a medal hopeful. In the 1902 World Figure Skating Championships, Madge was the first woman to compete in what had always been a male event. In fact, a women's event at the Olympics was created as a direct result of her achievements. In 1906 and 1907 Madge won the ladies' events and went on to win the gold at the 1908 Summer Olympics. The judges had commented on   **10**
how excellent she was and that she was in a totally different class to all of the other competitors.

Madge Syers was fundamental in changing the sport of figure skating in the Olympics by becoming the first woman ever to win an Olympic gold in skating.

1   Where were the Olympic games held in 1908?

_____

2   Give **TWO** reasons why Madge Syers was remarkable.

_____

_____

What do these words mean as used in the text?

3   hosted (line 3)   _____

4   aquatics (line 4)   _____

5   hopeful (line 6)   _____

Select the **ONE** word on the right that has the most **SIMILAR** meaning to the word on the left. Underline the correct answer.

6 fault   **a** question   **b** test   **c** flaw   **d** perfect   **e** uncommon

7 foe   **a** mistake   **b** fighter   **c** partner   **d** friend   **e** enemy

8 famous   **a** known   **b** noun   **c** no   **d** now   **e** own

9 festival   **a** meal   **b** sport   **c** carnival   **d** birthday   **e** sedentary

---

Select the **TWO** odd words out on each line. Select your answers by underlining **TWO** of the options **a–e**.

0   **a** slender   **b** thin   **c** narrow   **d** broad   **e** wide

1   **a** poem   **b** story   **c** drama   **d** book   **e** pamphlet

2   **a** creep   **b** speed   **c** rush   **d** crawl   **e** dash

3   **a** app   **b** game   **c** download   **d** mobile   **e** phone

---

These sentences have been jumbled up and all have **ONE** extra word. Underline the word that is not needed.

4   toast my under on marmalade love I

5   birds winter holiday migrate in many the

6   the island sand the pirates on buried treasure of chest the

Test 17: **Missing Letters**

In each of the following words there are some letters missing. Complete each word by selecting the missing letters from options **a–e** to make a word that has an **OPPOSITE** meaning to the word on the left.

Example: start   f __ n __ s __   (finish)

a ies   **b** ish   **c** eat   **d** <u>iih</u>   **e** ait

1 ugly   b __ a __ t __ f __ l

    a etau   **b** euiu   **c** euia   **d** eueu   **e** eilu

2 tiny   __ n __ r __ o __ s

    a iomu   **b** eomu   **c** eoma   **d** iomo   **e** eumu

3 young   m __ t __ r __

    a aue   **b** aie   **c** eue   **d** eie   **e** aoe

4 quiet   __ o __ s __

    a tiy   **b** nis   **c** rue   **d** niy   **e** noe

5 dyed   b __ e __ c __ e __

    a enld   **b** leer   **c** lahd   **d** rahd   **e** rahe

6 lend   __ o __ r __ w

    a tmo   **b** cno   **c** mro   **d** sro   **e** bro

Find the missing four letters that need to be added to these words so that the sentence makes sense. The four letters do not have to make a word.

Example: I have great r_____m so I love to dance.

a ithe   **b** itit   **c** <u>hyth</u>   **d** hith   **e** itth

7 Alfie visited the dentist as he had too _____ he.

   a that   **b** tcac   **c** tcat   **d** thac   **e** chac

8 Stanley sailed his yacht on the bo _____ g lake.

   a oati   **b** oath   **c** ooti   **d** atti   **e** atin

9 Mum bought the twins a ba _____ n each from the summer fair.

   a loon   **b** lloo   **c** leoo   **d** llou   **e** llow

0 The hill had been the site of a f _____ s civil war battle.

   a ameu   **b** ameo   **c** amou   **d** amoo   **e** aymo

---

Find the three-letter word that is needed to complete each word so that each sentence makes sense. The missing three letters must make a word.

     4

Example: The boy pedalled his b _____ cle up the hill.

   a act   **b** <u>icy</u>   **c** lay   **d** air   **e** ice

1 There was lots of our fav _____ ite food at the meal.

   a are   **b** ire   **c** air   **d** our   **e** use

2 Our school day ends at qu _____ er past three.

   a arc   **b** ark   **c** art   **d** can   **e** con

3 We use an excla _____ ion mark at the end of some sentences.

   a tag   **b** vat   **c** mat   **d** met   **e** mut

4 Mum worked hard as she owned her own _____ iness.

   a bus   **b** bet   **c** car   **d** cur   **e** tat

Test 18: **Comprehension**

Read the text carefully and then answer the questions that follow.

The Treehouse

Mum and Dad sighed with relief. Grandad had picked up Rufus and Hal and they had the house to themselves for the weekend. They had so much to do, but they were prepared. First of all they opened the garage and dragged out planks of wood. Mum began measuring carefully and then sawing the planks to size. Dad began pruning the tree, just where it was needed. Dad then took **5** the planks of cut wood and drilled and screwed the pieces together, following the plan that Mum had carefully designed. Once the wooden frame was built, Dad began varnishing the outside while Mum decorated the inside. Little shelves went up, a row of hooks for coats, a tabletop for playing, a chest for storing board games, beanbag seats for relaxing and finally, a pair of identical, **10** comfortable, squishy, squashy beds.

The boys returned on Sunday afternoon ready for their birthday tea. Mum and Dad could hardly keep awake, but they could not wait to show the boys their present. Leading them down the garden path, Mum and Dad took the two boys and then watched their faces as the twins took in the most handsome, **15** exciting, beautiful treehouse.

The two boys could not believe their eyes. It took just seconds before they scrambled up the ladder and into their new playroom. They lay on the beds, opened the cubby holes, sat on the beanbag seats and marvelled at the space. This was the best birthday present ever. **20**

1 Why did Mum and Dad build the boys a treehouse?

_____

_____

2 How do you think Mum and Dad felt at the end of the text? Give **THREE** answers, using the text to support each one.

_____

_____

_____

_____

_____

Test continues after Answers section →

Answers

Test 1: Comprehension

1 The women were herding the goats and sheep up the mountainside.

2 When it was less hot, the goats climbed the argan trees to eat the argan fruit.

3 1 mark each for referring to any three of the following: she felt happy to be away from the bustle and noise; she felt relieved that the cold floor has soothed her hot feet; she could relax away from the persistent sunlight; she appreciated the scented air and freshness away from the hot dirt path; she felt calm hearing the trickling water instead of the noise and bustle.

4 Fatima couldn't resist the sticky dates and wanted to eat some when she returned home.

5 'Searing' means very hot or boiling.

6 'Merciless' means without mercy or respite.

7 'Bustle' means hectic activity and movement.

8 'Bulging' means totally full, expanded or swollen.

9 'Dates that were clumped together like pyramids' is a simile.

10 'Leaving the soles of her feet on fire' is a metaphor.

11 'The merciless sun' is personification.

Test 2: Missing Words

1 manically
2 gripped
3 tugged
4 clattered
5 perplexed
6 unwise
7 ant
8 bat
9 one
10 has
11 e museum
12 c relieved
13 c orchard

14 d plane
15 d audience

Test 3: Matching Words

1	a motivate	10	d	expected
2	b disturb	11	d	rash
3	d beat	12	d	deliberate
4	b increase	13	e	shortened
5	e accomplish	14	c	built
6	e recognised	15	c	charged
7	c destroy	16	a	nervously
8	d historic	17	d	occupation
9	e unite	18	e	kind

Test 4: Mixed

1 e It states that 'Molly had always wanted to be a mechanical engineer'.

2 c It states that Molly had 'changed her mind' from following her father; e it states that Molly was 'painstaking in her approach'.

3 c It states that Molly had 'found a cure', which is good news.

4 hot
5 tie
6 won
7 den
8 a view
9 c rest
10 d droop
11 c newest
12 a search

Test 5: Missing Letters

1 b, d (There were some attractive pictures on the calendar.)

2 b, d (Solomon's new hairstyle was very fashionable.)

3 d, c (Ellie put up some shelving to store her ornaments.)

4 d, b (The train hurtled past the little snow-covered villages en route to the mountains.)

5 c tnes (witness)

6 b geth (together)

7 c houg (although)

8 c tant (substantial)

9 d IBRA (library)

10 b OTAT (potatoes)

11 a PLAI (complaining)

12 a ASCA (cascaded)

13 e TREM (extremely)

Test 6: Missing Words

1 d material

2 c busy

3 b annual

4 d disappear

5 c circumnavigated

6 b looking after

7 c she was

8 d was looking

9 a with clusters

10 d it is

11 b den

12 a nag

13 b and

14 d jam

15 b ear

Test 7: Matching Words

1 i ordinary, **u** normal

2 a depart, **o** go

3 g pause, **w** halt

4 e legendary, **s** famous

5 t turn, **x** rotate

6 e competition

7 c drink

8 e confirmed

9 a remember

10 e intense

11 c progress

12 a assortment

13 d needed

14 c happen

15 c bend

Test 8: Mixed

1 b, d (It became apparent that Year 6 needed more help with their grammar.)

2 d, b (Wait before getting something until you know how much you really want it.)

3 c, d (The King's soldiers prepared for battle.)

4 b, e (Wilma buttoned up her cardigan and straightened her tie.)

5 d dictionary

6 a some

7 d lightning

8 b notorious

9 uic (quicken, quickly)

10 tur (pasture, turnips)

11 evi (television, revision)

12 ark (sparkle, remarkable)

13 zzl (puzzles, sizzling)

14 a drooping

15 e commiserate

16 a incorporate

Test 9: Comprehension

1 c The text refers to Gabriel shaking a tin and collecting coins, and at the end he gives the money to the charity coordinator.

2 a It states that 'he couldn't let down a little girl'

3 c It states that 'Gabriel looked in horror'.

4 b busy

5 c produce

6 e triumphed

7 e tried

Test 10: Missing Words

1 holiday

2 gaggle

3 Peering

4 impatience

5 waddled

6 convinced

7 honking

8 chaos

9 expressions

0 realised

1 ate

2 rat

3 war

4 lid

5 b constructed

6 d snow

7 e visit

est 11: Missing Letters

1 q e t o (question)

2 o i o t l (horizontal)

3 d e d u (dreadful)

4 e i n (lenient)

5 p e u i e (prejudiced)

6 s e o (boisterous)

7 citi (exciting)

8 resh (refreshment)

9 iden (confidence)

0 hine (machines)

1 entu (eventually)

12 rkne (darkness)

13 hron (throne)

14 ened (opened)

15 aut (beautiful)

16 ied (hurriedly)

17 cte (neglected)

18 str (orchestra)

19 nni (beginning)

20 olo (technology)

21 ndo (tremendous)

22 nti (frantically)

est 12: Mixed

1 1 mark for referring to 'saving life' or being an 'important aspect of first aid'.

2 1 mark each for any three of the following: it includes statistics; it includes a diagram; it includes a quote; it gives information on how to do something; it is informative.

3 You should check that it is clear so that they can breathe.

4 c, b (The quiet night was peaceful and still.)

5 d, a (A robotic limb can be used when it would be treacherous to use a person.)

6 d, b (The singer tweeted that the band had written a new album.)

7 c, a (There was a huge audience at the cinema for the latest film release.)

8 e, a (We spent the afternoon creating homemade decorations.)

9 c, d (We were able to fly from our regional airport when we began our journey to Portugal.)

Test 13: Comprehension

1 d The text states that his appearance was 'nothing of note', he was 'instantly forgettable' and that 'nobody realised that he was the entertainment'.

2 b It states that the audience were 'mesmerized'.

3 d reversing (the spelling rule is to take off the 'e' before adding 'ing')

4 d hypnotic, artistic, nondescript

5 b beautiful

6 c changed

7 a enthusiastically

8 c talented

9 a captivated

Test 14: Matching Words

1 a impersonate

2 c snatch

3 a neglected

4 a gather

5 c keg

6 d set

7 e amending

8 b contest

9 c beaten

10 a heir

11 c tune

12 b unchanging

13 c fight

14 a attraction

15 b roast, **d** bake

16 a early, **d** punctual

17 b grasping, **e** greedy

18 c tiresome, **e** tedious

19 a tassel, **d** fringe

20 a property, **b** possessions

Test 15: Missing Words

1 aquarium (We bought a new kennel for our dog. / We bought a kennel for our new dog.)
2 mechanic (The dance studio put on a wonderful show.)
3 cakes (We had vegetable sauce with our pasta. / We had pasta with our vegetable sauce.)
4 wind (The rain was so heavy that the water flooded the street.)
5 after (He took a deep breath before swimming underwater. / Before swimming underwater he took a deep breath.)
6 base (The house stood on the corner of the street.)
7 **c** capital
8 **b** square
9 **a** highlight
10 **d** horizon
11 **e** steered
12 **e** hoped
13 bears
14 berries
15 plump
16 ripe
17 exports
18 producer

Test 16: Mixed

1 1 mark for London or UK.
2 (1 mark) she was the first woman to compete in a male event; (1 mark) she won an Olympic gold medal in figure skating.
3 'Hosted' means held, presented or ran.
4 'Aquatics' means water sports.
5 'Hopeful' means someone with a good chance of winning.
6 **c** flaw
7 **e** enemy
8 **a** known
9 **c** carnival
10 **d** broad, **e** wide
11 **d** book, **e** pamphlet

12 **a** creep, **d** crawl
13 **d** mobile, **e** phone
14 under (I love marmalade on my toast.)
15 holiday (Many birds migrate in the winter.)
16 sand (The pirates buried the chest of treasure on the island.)

Test 17: Missing Letters

1 **b** e u i u (beautiful)
2 **b** e o m u (enormous)
3 **a** a u e (mature)
4 **d** n i y (noisy)
5 **c** l a h d (bleached)
6 **e** b r o (borrow)
7 **d** thac (toothache)
8 **e** atin (boating)
9 **b** lloo (balloon)
10 **c** amou (famous)
11 **d** our
12 **c** art
13 **c** mat
14 **a** bus

Test 18: Comprehension

1 It was a birthday present. The text states it 'was the best birthday present ever'.
2 1 mark each for any of the following reasons with their supporting examples from the text: tired (Mum and Dad could hardly keep awake); excited/eager (they could not wait to show the boys); nervous (then watched their faces).
3 1 mark each for any three of the following reasons: reading (books could go on the shelves); playing games (a chest for storing board games); playing with toys (a tabletop for playing); relaxing (beanbags for relaxing); sleeping (beds).
4 'Pruning' means chopping or cutting branches off the tree.
5 'Identical' means exactly the same.
6 'Handsome' means good- or fine-looking.
7 'Scrambled' means climbed.

8 'Marvelled' means looked in admiration or wonder.

9 The phrase 'could not believe their eyes' means they were amazed by what they saw.

Test 19: Missing Words

1 sum

2 art

3 mat

4 owe

5 key

6 art

7 grooming

8 relationship

9 saddle

10 prepared

11 unbalanced

12 boot

13 reins

14 **e** decided

15 **a** people

16 **c** pharmacist

17 **c** peak

18 **a** cross

19 **d** courses

Test 20: Mixed

1 **d** p c o s (spacious)

2 **b** a u l (casual)

3 **e** b t e (bitter)

4 **c** p u a (plural)

5 **e** f s i a i g (fascinating)

6 **b** atio (station)

7 **d** lour (colourful)

8 **c** avyw (heavyweight)

9 **b** lodd (plodded)

10 **a** ajes (majestic)

11 **c** spir (inspired)

12 ale, lop

13 for, low

14 van, cat

15 tin, one

16 ice, ant

Test 21: Matching Words

1 **b** wound

2 **c** separating

3 **c** slept

4 **d** dancing

5 **d** nourished

6 **e** blossoming

7 **d** defend

8 **d** narrow

9 **d** worthless

10 **a** bottom, **i** base

11 **h** pale, **p** fair

12 **e** flinch, **x** wince

13 **t** funny, **v** amusing

14 **d** single, **w** solo

15 **m** speed, **s** haste

Test 22: Comprehension

1 **c** The text states that it is the 'only place where some endangered plants and butterflies can still be found'.

d It states that it is 'ideal for people with an interest in history'.

2 **b** The text states that the Cotswolds stretch 'from south of' Stratford-upon-Avon, which does not include the town itself.

d It states that the limestone is 'rich in fossils'.

3 **c** Beverston Castle and Sudeley Castle are ideal for people with an interest in history.

4 **c** amazing

5 **d** approximately

6 **c** special

7 **d** plentiful

8 **b** threatened

9 **b** The text is factual. The text is informative.

Test 23: Missing Words

1 **c** canteen (The new books had arrived in the school library.)

2 **a** sung (We made an anti-bullying poster in school today. / Today in school we made an anti-bullying poster. / In school today we made an anti-bullying poster.)

3 **a** sleep (Jack had a drum lesson on Wednesday afternoon. / On Wednesday afternoon Jack had a drum lesson.)

4 **b** tomato (Mum likes to pour cream on her fruit salad.)

5 **c** weak, **e** feeble

6 **b** arrive, **d** come

7 **a** arid, **b** dry

8 **b** owl, **c** eagle

9 **a** square, **d** box

10 **e** protect

11 **a** stray

12 **c** perimeter

13 **b** relieved

14 **b** important

15 **b** are, **a** air

16 **d** rot, **b** bat

17 **d** lie, **c** lid

Test 24: Mixed

1 u i u (curious)

2 e c m n (welcoming)

3 s i k n (stinking)

4 n h n i g (enchanting)

5 p r l (spiral)

6 d a t g (advantage)

7 **c** expand

8 **e** extra

9 **c** turned

10 **b** pushed

11 **a** COLA (chocolate)

12 **d** COLO (colourful)

13 **e** EWSP (newspaper)

14 **b** CINE (cinema)

15 **a** ill, **b** poorly

16 **a** flour, **d** butter

17 **d** ball, **e** bat

18 **a** iron, **c** smooth

19 **b** fluffy, **e** soft

Test 25: Matching Words

1 **c** stumbled

2 **b** scraped

3 **b** uncovered

4 **c** hidden

5 **d** following

6 **c** normally

7 **b** revolving

8 **d** jolly

9 **b** proud

10 **b** test

11 **d** droopy

12 **h** heated, **x** fiery

13 **e** low, **t** short

14 **f** creative, **l** original

15 **d** intelligent, **u** bright

Test 26: Comprehension

1 She told him that he mustn't mess about in the new bathroom.

2 1 mark each for any two of the following: he copied Mum's words; he shook his finger at his reflection; he made a toothpaste snake.

3 Impishness or naughtiness made him do something he knew he shouldn't do.

4 The toothpaste looked like a big, fat, minty slug.

5 Jake's handiwork was a bathroom sink full of toothpaste.

6 1 mark for each of the following points: Jake had done what Mum had asked him not to, so he would be in trouble; Jake could not get the toothpaste back into the tube.

7 1 mark each for any two of the following reasons and 1 mark for each reason why: Jake felt guilty (he had done what Mum had asked him not to); Jake felt worried (his mum was about to come in and see what he had done); Jake was frustrated (he couldn't get the toothpaste back into the tube); Jake felt panic (he knew he was about to be found out); Jake felt scared (Mum was going to come in angry and he might be grounded or made to tidy his room).

Test 27: Missing Letters

1 **b** ATEF (plateful)

2 **d** INGE (ginger)

3 **c** OUGH (bought)

4 c EAUT (beautiful)

5 b i i h (finish)

6 d e c i g (teaching)

7 c s o t d (spotted)

8 a o s s e (possessed)

9 e a g r u (dangerous)

10 d d c r t d (decorated)

11 c u i u (furious)

12 d u m r e (submerged)

13 b e t r d (textured)

Test 28: Mixed

1 a England (There are twelve sovereign states in South America.)

2 b drown (The boat rocked violently on the stormy sea.)

3 a hearing, **c** sight

4 a multiply, **b** times

5 b polished

6 c useful

7 c squirting

8 b simple

9 d vacation

10 d total

11 e snooze

12 b supporter, **h** buff

13 e specific, **s** precise

14 w manage, **x** cope

Test 29: Mixed

1 a The text states that Orwell wrote novels.

c Orwell dressed like a homeless person.

2 c The text states that Orwell explored poverty 'as a social experiment' and 'wrote up these experiences'.

3 brass

4 orchestra

5 instrument

6 modern

7 combination

8 notes

9 c sham

10 a dare

11 b infinite

12 a aim

Test 30: Mixed

1 c, b (The choir sang at the sheltered retirement home.)

2 d, b (The pool was cool and invigorating after such hot weather.)

3 e crushed

4 c stained

5 a still

6 c bright

7 b enthusiastic

8 c lucky

9 c silky, **s** smooth

10 k fair, **v** level

11 g labour, **j** toil

12 m ascend, **y** rise

Test 31: Mixed

1 ana (management, anagrams)

2 emb (assembly, embarrassment)

3 ili (possibility, facility)

4 b lebr (celebrity)

5 d enda (calendar)

6 d quir (squirrel)

7 d sea, **e** ocean

8 c van, **e** bus

9 d obtuse, **e** fat

10 b jumped

11 e happily

12 d wrote

13 b present

14 b unwanted

15 b packaging

16 e astronaut

17 a extraterrestrial

PUZZLE ANSWERS

Puzzle 1

Trees: pine, oak, elm, ash, birch, beech, willow, holly, sycamore, hazel, apple, cherry

Flowers: rose, tulip, daisy, daffodil, iris, crocus, bluebell, honeysuckle, lily, snowdrop, primrose, foxglove

Puzzle 2

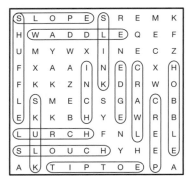

creep, crawl, slink, skulk, slope, tiptoe, edge, inch, shuffle, hobble, slouch, waddle, lurch

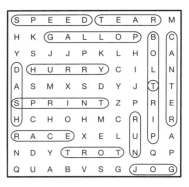

race, speed, hurry, dash, sprint, run, gallop, canter, tear, trip, bolt, trot, jog

Puzzle 3

New words: pigeon, soup, attend, teabag, toothbrush, snowman, season, redcurrant, landslide

Puzzle 4

hour, our; dye, die; reign, rein, rain; no, know; buy, by, bye; sew, so, sow; yew, ewe, you; read, red, reed; meet, meat; led, lead; steel, steal; reel, real; their, there; tire, tyre; dew, due; aloud, allowed; rung, wrung; sale, sail; seen, scene; made, maid; lessen, lesson; feint, faint; floor, flaw; find, fined; stair, stare

Puzzle 5

Big: huge, vast, enormous, massive, gigantic

Small: tiny, little, minuscule, minute, miniature

Tasty: delicious, tempting, succulent, scrumptious, appetizing

Inedible: disgusting, revolting, sickly, bitter, unpalatable

Puzzle 6

List 6: pale, white, wan, bleached, ashen

Puzzle 7

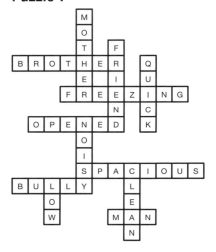

Puzzle 8

Other examples are fine. Here are some suggestions:

B: bear, Ben, broccoli, Bernadette, barley, basketbal

C: cow, Charles, curry, Cathy, chrysanthemum, chess

F: fox, Fred, figs, Freya, foxglove, fencing

G: giraffe, Gerard, grapefruit, Gemma, gladioli, golf

H: hedgehog, Hashmee, honey, Hannah, holly, horse-riding

K: kangaroo, Kevin, kiwi, Keisha, knotweed, knitting

L: lion, Leo, lasagne, Leah, lily, lace-making

M: mouse, Mickey, mango, Michelle, marigold, macramé

3 Find **THREE** kinds of activities that Rufus and Hal could do in their treehouse, based on the text.

⬭ 3

_____

_____

_____

What do these words mean as used in the text?

⬭ 5

4 pruning (line 5)   _____

5 identical (line 10)   _____

6 handsome (line 15)   _____

7 scrambled (line 18)   _____

8 marvelled (line 19)   _____

9 What does the phrase 'could not believe their eyes' (line 17) mean?

⬭ 1

_____

_____

Total ⬜ 13

Test 19: **Missing Words**

Find the three-letter word that is needed to complete each word so that each sentence makes sense. The missing three letters must make a word.

Example: The boy pedalled his b___*icy*___cle up the hill. (bicycle)

1   At the end of the _____ mer's day, the sunset was glorious.

2   The little fish swam quickly, d_____ing this way, then that way.

3   We butter the bread and then layer cheese, to_____o and cucumber.

4   The girl foll_____d the butterfly as it flew around the garden.

5   In Japan, there are mon_____s who sit on the back of deer who happily provide a lift.

6   It is called symbiotic when animals live in a happy p_____nership.

Read the following paragraph and add one word from the list to each space so that the paragraph makes sense. There are more words than there are spaces so some will be left out, but each word can only be used once.

boot	grooming	horse	prepared	reins
relationship	relaxed	saddle	securely	unbalanced

7–13   It is useful to get to know your horse first of all, so _____

is a good way of building a _____ with your horse as well

as making sure there is no dirt underneath the _____.

Once your horse is saddled and _____, mount up and then

prepare to walk on. At first, you might feel a little _____ in

the saddle, but good posture and sitting in the correct position is vital. There should be a straight line from your shoulder, down through your elbow, down to your hip

and to the heel of your _____. As you walk on, keep your

head looking forward with your arms relaxed at your sides, the elbows bent. Make

sure that you are sitting securely balanced in the saddle. Don't swing your legs or

turn them outwards, and hold the _____ lightly.

Choose **ONE** word that is the best fit in each of these sentences. Underline your
answer from options **a–e**.

6

14   Lucy _____ to walk home after school.

    a couldn't   **b** learn   **c** pupil   **d** want   **e** decided

15   Stir-up Sunday is when many _____ make their Christmas pudding.

    a people   **b** teachers   **c** elves   **d** children   **e** friends

16   The _____ gave Mum a bottle of medicine for my cough.

    a chemical   **b** chemistry   **c** pharmacist   **d** queen   **e** vet

17   From the _____ of the mountain you could see five counties.

    a base   **b** median   **c** peak   **d** peep   **e** pip

18   The team tried to work together so that they could all _____ the river safely.

    a cross   **b** across   **c** move   **d** bridge   **e** together

19   The medieval feast consisted of many food _____.

    a parts   **b** segments   **c** sections   **d** courses   **e** pieces

Total   19

Test 20: **Mixed**

In each of the following words there are some letters missing. Complete each word by selecting the missing letters from options **a–e** to make a word that has an **OPPOSITE** meaning to the word on the left.

1 cramped   s __ a __ i __ u __

 a ptos   **b** pshs   **c** phus   **d** pcos   **e** psos

2 formal   c __ s __ a __

 a asl   **b** aul   **c** ahl   **d** ael   **e** awl

3 sweet   __ i __ t __ r

 a bne   **b** pte   **c** mte   **d** nte   **e** bte

4 singular   __ l __ r __ l

 a cou   **b** fua   **c** pua   **d** pou   **e** sou

5 tedious   __ a __ c __ n __ t __ n __

 a faiaig   **b** fciaig   **c** fsiaag   **d** fseaig   **e** fsiaig

Find the missing four letters that need to be added to these words so that the sentence makes sense. The four letters do not have to make a word.

6 The train st_____n was adjacent to the shopping centre.

 a aito   **b** atio   **c** into   **d** itan   **e** anti

7 The arboretum had some co_____ful plants and shrubs.

 a louw   **b** lerf   **c** louf   **d** lour   **e** leur

8 The he_____eight boxer visited the sports centre last weekend.

   a evyl   **b** avyl   **c** avyw   **d** evyw   **e** aviw

9 The camels p_____ed carefully along the desert track.

   a rowv   **b** lodd   **c** rodd   **d** ludd   **e** ruvd

10 The peaks of the m_____tic mountains were snow-covered all year round.

   a ajes   **b** aget   **c** agne   **d** init   **e** orel

11 'The Lady of Shalott' is a poem that has in_____ed paintings by many artists.

   a spar   **b** sper   **c** spir   **d** spyr   **e** spur

---

Find the three-letter word that is needed to complete each word so that each sentence makes sense. The missing three letters must make a word. The two three-letter words needed for each sentence must be different.

10

12 Jon typed the letter and then se_____d it in the enve_____e.

13 The trees in the _____est had autumnal leaves of yel_____ and orange.

14 Cara_____s in a popular lo_____ion are a common type of holiday accommodation.

15 The musicians recorded the track, dona_____g the

   m_____y to charity.

16 The whole school had a magnif_____nt trip to the theatre to

   see a p_____omime.

Total   21

Test 21: **Matching Words**

Read the following sentences and answer the questions with the most sensible word.

'The path snaked around the house before dividing the lawn from the lake.'

1 What does the word 'snaked' mean as used in the sentence?

    a hurt   **b** wound   **c** hissed   **d** crept   **e** jumped

2 What does the word 'dividing' mean as used in the sentence?

    a sharing   **b** multiplying   **c** separating   **d** snipping   **e** timing

'The cat napped in front of the flickering flames of the fire.'

3 What does the word 'napped' mean as used in the sentence?

    a lay   **b** sat   **c** slept   **d** twitched   **e** washed

4 What does the word 'flickering' mean as used in the sentence?

    a hot   **b** cool   **c** friendly   **d** dancing   **e** smooth

'She fed the plants until they rewarded her with blooming flowers.'

5 What does the word 'fed' mean as used in the sentence?

    a grew   **b** snacked   **c** ignored   **d** nourished   **e** potted

6 What does the word 'blooming' mean as used in the sentence?

    a white   **b** shining   **c** bright   **d** colourful   **e** blossoming

---

Select the **ONE** word on the right that has the most **OPPOSITE** meaning to the word on the left. Underline the correct answer.

7 attack   **a** shoot   **b** hit   **c** guide   **d** defend   **e** lead

8 broad   **a** wide   **b** low   **c** tall   **d** narrow   **e** edging

9 precious   **a** ring   **b** gem   **c** dislike   **d** worthless   **e** moody

Look at the words in the grid and then use them to answer the questions.

a bottom	b pair	c break	d single	e flinch
f glue	g black	h pale	i base	j crash
k stick	l might	m speed	n paste	o pole
p fair	q adhere	r double	s haste	t funny
u power	v amusing	w solo	x wince	y couple

0 Find **TWO** words that are **OPPOSITE** to the word 'top'.

_____   _____

1 Find **TWO** words that are **OPPOSITE** to the word 'dark'.

_____   _____

2 Find **TWO** words that are most **SIMILAR** to the word 'jump'.

_____   _____

3 Find **TWO** words that are most **SIMILAR** to the word 'comical'.

_____   _____

4 Find **TWO** words that are **OPPOSITE** to the word 'multiple'.

_____   _____

5 Find **TWO** words that are most **SIMILAR** to the word 'quickness'.

_____   _____

Test 22: **Comprehension**

Read the text carefully and then answer the questions that follow.

The Cotswolds

The golden Cotswold stone is used to build many of the houses within the area of the Cotswolds – an Area of Outstanding Natural Beauty. The area itself is roughly 145 kilometres long by 40 kilometres wide, stretching from south of Shakespeare's Stratford-upon-Avon to an area south of Bath. The Cotswolds are situated mainly within the counties of Gloucestershire and Oxfordshire, although other counties also form parts of the area.   5

The area is made up of a number of very attractive villages and small towns, from Cheltenham and Broadway to Chipping Norton and Stroud. They are built over a type of limestone that is rich in fossils. This limestone and the grasslands that cover it form an important habitat. It is the only place where   10 some endangered plants and butterflies can still be found.

There are many exceptional places to visit in the Cotswolds. Sudeley Castle and Beverston Castle are ideal for people with an interest in history, as are Cheltenham with its Georgian architecture and the Roman town of Cirencester. If gardens are of more interest, the garden at Corsham Court, designed by Capability Brown, is   15 delightful. Whatever your interests, the Cotswolds are certain not to disappoint.

1   Select the **TWO** true statements. Underline the correct answers.

   a   The Cotswolds consist of just two counties.

   b   All of the houses in the Cotswolds are made of golden coloured stone.

   c   There is some rare and unusual nature found in the Cotswolds.

   d   People with an interest in the past would enjoy visiting the Cotswolds.

   e   Corsham Castle has a garden designed by Capability Brown.

2   Select the **TWO** false statements. Underline the correct answers.

   a   The Romans were in the Cotswolds.

   b   Shakespeare lived in the Cotswolds.

   c   Stroud is a village or town in the Cotswolds.

   d   The limestone in the Cotswolds has very few fossils in it.

   e   The Cotswolds is an area of natural beauty.

3 Which **TWO** places should you visit if you like history? Underline the correct answer. ⬭ 2

  a Corsham Court and Beverston Castle

  b Cheltenham and Sudeley Castle

  c Beverston Castle and Sudeley Castle

  d Sudeley Castle and Cheltenham

  e Capability Brown and Cirencester

Underline **ONE** word on the right that is closest in meaning to the word on the left, as it is used in the text. ⬭ 5

4 outstanding (line 2) **a** debt **b** minimal **c** amazing **d** unsettling

5 roughly (line 3) **a** evenly **b** bumpy **c** unevenly **d** approximately

6 exceptional (line 12) **a** awful **b** funny **c** special **d** ordinary

7 rich (line 9) **a** wealthy **b** worthy **c** lacking **d** plentiful

8 endangered (line 11) **a** dangerous **b** threatened **c** extinct **d** harmful

9 Underline the option that correctly describes this text. ⬭ 1

  a The text is fictional. The text is humorous.

  b The text is factual. The text is informative.

  c The text is informative. The text is fictional.

Total 12

Test 23: **Missing Words**

These sentences have been jumbled up and all have **ONE** extra word. Select the extra word in each of the sentences by underlining **ONE** word from options **a–e**.

Example: so cream eat the were cakes delicious

             (The cream cakes were so delicious.)

a cakes   **b** the   **c** <u>eat</u>   **d** were   **e** cream

1   library arrived in the canteen new books school had the

     a library   **b** arrived   **c** canteen   **d** books   **e** school

2   sung today school poster in made anti-bullying we an

     a sung   **b** school   **c** poster   **d** made   **e** an

3   Wednesday afternoon sleep Jack drum had a lesson on

     a sleep   **b** drum   **c** had   **d** lesson   **e** on

4   pour tomato salad on her fruit likes Mum cream to

     a pour   **b** tomato   **c** salad   **d** fruit   **e** cream

---

Select the **TWO** odd words out on each line. Select your answers by underlining **TWO** of the options **a–e**.

Example: **a** friend   **b** companion   **c** <u>compact</u>   **d** <u>converted</u>   **e** buddy

5 **a** strong   **b** rigid   **c** weak   **d** powerful   **e** feeble

6 **a** leave   **b** arrive   **c** depart   **d** come   **e** go

7 **a** arid   **b** dry   **c** moist   **d** damp   **e** wet

8 **a** starling   **b** owl   **c** eagle   **d** robin   **e** blackbird

9 **a** square   **b** heart   **c** liver   **d** box   **e** lung

Choose **ONE** word that is the best fit in each of these sentences. Underline your answer from options **a–e**.

5

10 Farmer Frank put up new fencing to _____ his animals.

a allow   **b** permit   **c** welcome   **d** free   **e** protect

11 He was worried that his animals might _____.

a stray   **b** gain   **c** curb   **d** limit   **e** run

12 He added extra fencing to secure the _____ of the farm.

a side   **b** aria   **c** perimeter   **d** field   **e** space

13 Once he had finished this big job, he felt _____.

a sad   **b** relieved   **c** exquisite   **d** temperamental   **e** bored

14 The safety of his animals was so _____ to him.

a irrelevant   **b** important   **c** lovely   **d** irresponsible   **e** irritating

---

Find the three-letter word that is needed to complete each word so that each sentence makes sense. The missing three letters must make a word. Underline the **TWO** answers needed from options **a–e**.

6

Example: I am just pop_____g to the shop to buy some fur_____ure polish.

a pan   **b** <u>pin</u>   **c** pun   **d** net   **e** <u>nit</u>

15 The children were in the pool as their p_____nts sat on deckch_____s.

a air   **b** are   **c** err   **d** our   **e** owe

16 To p_____ect their skin from the sun, the sun_____hers wore suntan lotion.

a bar   **b** bat   **c** bay   **d** rot   **e** rut

17 Each of the fami_____s had a wonderful ho_____ay.

a lad   **b** lay   **c** lid   **d** lie   **e** lye

Total   20

Test 24: **Mixed**

Add the missing letters to the word on the right to make a word with a **SIMILAR** meaning to the word on the left.

1 inquisitive   c __ r __ o __ s

2 friendly   w __ l __ o __ i __ g

3 smelly   __ t __ n __ i __ g

4 captivating   e __ c __ a __ t __ n __

5 coil   s __ i __ a __

6 bonus   a __ v __ n __ a __ e

Read the following sentences and answer the questions with the most sensible word.

'Stretch the batter mixture a little further by adding additional fruit.'

7 What does the word 'stretch' mean as used in the sentence?
   a contract   **b** abbreviate   **c** expand   **d** bounce   **e** bend

8 What does the word 'additional' mean as used in the sentence?
   a many   **b** plus   **c** plump   **d** big   **e** extra

'Shilpa rotated the wheel and fed the wool into the machine.'

9 What does the word 'rotated' mean as used in the sentence?
   a dropped   **b** paced   **c** turned   **d** oiled   **e** drew

10 What does the word 'fed' mean as used in the sentence?
   a dragged   **b** pushed   **c** pulled   **d** ate   **e** spooned

Find the missing four letters that need to be added to the letters in capitals to make a new word. The new word will complete the sentence sensibly. The four letters do not have to make a word.

4

1 There was a CHOTE egg hunt for children to participate in.
   a COLA   **b** COLE   **c** CERL   **d** CURI   **e** CLEA

2 Her hair was a URFUL mixture of purple, blue, red and orange.
   a VARI   **b** PRET   **c** BRIT   **d** COLO   **e** COLU

3 The NAPER edition ran the story about the newly opened park.
   a IRES   **b** AILT   **c** ARTT   **d** OWST   **e** EWSP

4 Grandad took us to the MA to see the latest film.
   a SINE   **b** CINE   **c** THEA   **d** FILA   **e** SIGN

Select the **TWO** odd words out on each line. Select your answers by underlining **TWO** of the options **a–e**.

5

5 **a** ill   **b** poorly   **c** well   **d** healthy   **e** fine

6 **a** flour   **b** cake   **c** biscuit   **d** butter   **e** cookie

7 **a** scooter   **b** bicycle   **c** skateboard   **d** ball   **e** bat

8 **a** iron   **b** fold   **c** smooth   **d** crease   **e** pleat

9 **a** fur   **b** fluffy   **c** hair   **d** hide   **e** soft

Total   19

Test 25: **Matching Words**

Read the following sentences and answer the questions with the most sensible word.

'Leo tripped and grazed his knee on the playground.

1   What does the word 'tripped' mean as used in the sentence?
  a holidayed   **b** travelled   **c** stumbled   **d** crumbled   **e** flipped

2   What does the word 'grazed' mean as used in the sentence?
  a glazed   **b** scraped   **c** scrapped   **d** bit   **e** pinched

'We unearthed the treasure that lay concealed for so many years.'

3   What does the word 'unearthed' mean as used in the sentence?
  a dug   **b** uncovered   **c** covered   **d** grew   **e** buried

4   What does the word 'concealed' mean as used in the sentence?
  a cold   **b** congealed   **c** hidden   **d** twinkling   **e** sealed

'The next day began typically with breakfast and the newspapers.'

5   What does the word 'next' mean as used in the sentence?
  a former   **b** latter   **c** previous   **d** following   **e** terminating

6   What does the word 'typically' mean as used in the sentence?
  a awkwardly   **b** sarcastically   **c** normally   **d** unusually   **e** rarely

'The rotating carousel played cheerful fairground music.'

7   What does the word 'rotating' mean as used in the sentence?
  a revolting   **b** revolving   **c** retiring   **d** reverting   **e** resplendent

8   What does the word 'cheerful' mean as used in the sentence?
  a colourful   **b** happiness   **c** special   **d** jolly   **e** grand

Select the **ONE** word on the right that has the most **SIMILAR** meaning to the word on the left. Underline the correct answer.

9 vain   **a** artery   **b** proud   **c** attractive   **d** unconfident   **e** afraid

0 trial   **a** offence   **b** test   **c** go   **d** trick   **e** prevent

1 slack   **a** tired   **b** sly   **c** tight   **d** droopy   **e** lack

Look at the words in the grid and then use them to answer the questions.

a shiny	**b** wide	**c** broad	**d** intelligent	**e** low
f creative	**g** long	**h** heated	**i** wise	**j** paid
k light	**l** original	**m** taper	**n** divided	**o** spoken
p reflective	**q** force	**r** spiced	**s** separate	**t** short
u bright	**v** friend	**w** work	**x** fiery	**y** said

2 Find **TWO** words that are **OPPOSITE** to the word 'cold'.

_____   _____

3 Find **TWO** words that are **OPPOSITE** to the word 'tall'.

_____   _____

4 Find **TWO** words that are most **SIMILAR** to the word 'imaginative'.

_____   _____

5 Find **TWO** words that are most **SIMILAR** to the word 'clever'.

_____   _____

Total   19

Read the text carefully and answer the questions that follow.

The Unfortunate Episode with the Toothpaste

"Don't mess about in the new bathroom," Mum shouted to Jake. Jake looked at himself in the new mirror that hung in the bathroom and copied his mum's words in a high-pitched voice while shaking a finger at his reflection. It made him laugh. He surveyed the room with little interest. Without thinking too much about it, he picked up the huge tube of new toothpaste and took off the cap. 5
He only meant to squeeze a tiny amount onto his toothbrush, but impishness gave him a brave edge and instead, he squeezed hard and a big, fat, minty slug appeared on his toothbrush bristles. "Eugh!" Jake thought in disgust. He squeezed really hard this time and a white phantom snake appeared to slither over the bristles and up the handle of the brush. Jake laughed at how funny 10
it looked. He shook his brush and toothpaste flew off the brush and into the new sink. Jake squeezed the tube again and again as he spelled his name out across the sink bowl. This was so much fun!

"Jake!" Mum yelled. "Are you in bed yet?" Jake came to his senses and looked at his handiwork. The huge tube of toothpaste was now three-quarters empty and the sink bowl was covered with toothpaste. Hurriedly, 15
Jake decided he needed to tidy up, so he began scooping up the toothpaste, ready to push it back into the tube, but try as he might, he could not get any toothpaste back into the tube. Jake began to panic, but nothing he did would get any of it back into the tube. He could hear Mum's footsteps 20
coming up the stairs, closer and closer. Jake could picture his mum's face and it would not be a happy face ...

1   What did Mum tell Jake he must not do?

_____

_____

2   Find **TWO** things that Jake did to make himself laugh.

_____

_____

3 What is meant by the phrase 'impishness gave him a brave edge' (line 7)?

_____

_____

4 Why did Jake feel disgust?

_____

_____

5 What was Jake's 'handiwork'?

_____

_____

6 Why did Jake panic? (line 19) Give **TWO** reasons.

_____

_____

_____

7 How do you think that Jake felt at the end of the text and why? Give **TWO** answers and support each by referring to the text.

_____

_____

_____

_____

Total ⬚ 12

Test 27: **Missing Letters**

Find the missing four letters that need to be added to the letters in capitals to make a new word. The new word will complete the sentence sensibly. The four letters do not have to make a word.

Example: I BHT a basket of tasty food to the picnic. (brought)

a OURT   **b** ROUG   **c** MIGH   **d** TRUT   **e** LOUH

1   We took a PLUL of sandwiches to the picnic.

    a AVEF   **b** ATEF   **c** ITEF   **d** ITIF   **e** ETIF

2   Mum had made some GR beer and homemade lemonade to take.

    a RAIN   **b** AMGE   **c** ANGE   **d** INGE   **e** IMGE

3   We BT a really large hutch for our guinea pigs.

    a RING   **b** RORT   **c** OUGH   **d** OOGH   **e** ORRE

4   There were BIFUL flowers overflowing from the hanging baskets.

    a YOUT   **b** EATI   **c** EAUT   **d** RIHT   **e** RITE

In each of the following words there are some letters missing. Complete each word by selecting the missing letters from options **a–e** to make a word most **SIMILAR** in meaning to the word on the left.

Example: supple   n __ m __ l __ (nimble)

a o a e   **b** a i e   **c** i b e   **d** e a e   **e** u a t

5   end   f __ n __ s __

    a o d e   **b** i i h   **c** e l e   **d** i e h   **e** i i i

6   coaching   t __ a __ h __ n __

    a e s a e   **b** r s i g   **c** e t i g   **d** e c i g   **e** e s i g

7 dotted   __ p __ t __ e __

   a o a r d   **b** o i u d   **c** s o t d   **d** a o i d   **e** a p i t

8 owned   p __ s __ e __ s __ d

   a o s s e   **b** a s s e   **c** o t s e   **d** a t s e   **e** a t a e

---

In each of the following words there are some letters missing. Complete each word by selecting the missing letters from the options **a–e** to make a word most **OPPOSITE** in meaning to the word on the left.

   5

Example: false   __ e __ u __ n __ (genuine)

   a <u>g n i e</u>   **b** j n i e   **c** g n a e   **d** j n a e   **e** g n e e

9 safe   d __ n __ e __ o __ s

   a a k n u   **b** a k r u   **c** o g r u   **d** e g r u   **e** a g r u

10 plain   __ e __ o __ a __ e __

   a f d r t d   **b** p t r c d   **c** n c r v d   **d** d c r t d   **e** r c n t d

11 calm   f __ r __ o __ s

   a a o e   **b** e r i   **c** u i u   **d** i i i   **e** u r u

12 floating   s __ b __ e __ g __ d

   a u b r e   **b** u m n e   **c** u b n e   **d** u m r e   **e** o m r e

13 smooth   t __ x __ u __ e __

   a e r d u   **b** e t r d   **c** e d r t   **d** e t u r   **e** u e d r

Total   13

Test 28: **Mixed**

These sentences have been jumbled up and all have **ONE** additional word. Select the extra word in each of the sentences by underlining **ONE** word from options **a–e**.

1   in sovereign England twelve states there are America South

    a England   **b** twelve   **c** states   **d** there   **e** are

2   rocked sea drown the violently the boat on stormy

    a stormy   **b** drown   **c** boat   **d** sea   **e** rocked

Select the **TWO** odd words out on each line. Select your answers by underlining **TWO** of the options **a–e**.

3   **a** hearing   **b** ear   **c** sight   **d** eye   **e** nose

4   **a** multiply   **b** times   **c** share   **d** divide   **e** split

Choose **ONE** word that is the best fit in each of these sentences. Underline your answer from options **a–e**.

5   The window cleaner washed, rinsed and then _____ the windows.

    a smeared   **b** polished   **c** purified   **d** cleansed   **e** shampooed

6   School spelling tests are a _____ way of focusing on spelling skills.

    a inefficient   **b** bad   **c** useful   **d** academic   **e** mean

7   The clown ran around the stage _____ water at the audience.

    a squishing   **b** squashing   **c** squirting   **d** squirrelling   **e** squirming

Select the **ONE** word on the right that has the most **SIMILAR** meaning to the word on the left. Underline the correct answer.

3   basic   **a** complicated   **b** simple   **c** satisfactory   **d** poorly   **e** first

9   holiday   **a** journey   **b** state   **c** vacancy   **d** vacation   **e** vacant

0   score   **a** team   **b** sport   **c** play   **d** total   **e** parade

1   nap   **a** bag   **b** sack   **c** nip   **d** wake   **e** snooze

---

Look at the words in the grid and then use them to answer the questions.

a enemy	**b** supporter	**c** might	**d** doubt	**e** specific
f pretend	**g** sunny	**h** buff	**i** sure	**j** wholly
k friend	**l** livid	**m** curtain	**n** struggle	**o** imaginary
p interest	**q** anger	**r** fight	**s** precise	**t** partially
u foe	**v** sport	**w** manage	**x** cope	**y** roughly

2   Find **TWO** words that are most **SIMILAR** to the word 'fan'.

_____   _____

3   Find **TWO** words that are **OPPOSITE** to the word 'vague'.

_____   _____

4   Find **TWO** words that are **OPPOSITE** to the word 'fail'.

_____   _____

Test 29: **Mixed**

Read the text carefully and answer the questions that follow.

George Orwell

In 1903 Eric Arthur Blair was born, although you will know him better by his writing name: George Orwell. He wrote essays, non-fiction books, newspaper and magazine columns, book reviews, poetry and novels.

As a social experiment, Orwell decided to explore the poverty in London by dressing like a homeless person and watching how people treated him when 　　　**5** he was poor. He then had a similar experience in Paris where he took on the job of washing dishes in a restaurant. He wrote up these experiences in the book *Down and Out in Paris and London*. Many years later, he wrote about the social conditions in the northwest of England in his book *The Road to Wigan Pier*. Orwell stayed in poor lodgings and took notes of the conditions in which 　　　**10** people were living.

Orwell spent time in Spain to fight in the Spanish Civil War. He was shot in the throat and was declared unfit for service on medical grounds. Back in England when the Second World War began, Orwell joined the Home Guard. In 1945 his novel *Animal Farm* was published and another novel, *Nineteen Eighty-* 　　　**15** *Four,* followed in 1949. Orwell's health declined and he was diagnosed with tuberculosis in 1947. He died in 1950.

1　Select the **TWO** true statements. Underline the correct answers.

  a　Orwell wrote fiction.

  b　Orwell fought in the French Civil War.

  c　Orwell sometimes pretended to live in poverty.

  d　Orwell wrote about the northeast of England.

  e　Orwell was in his fifties when he died.

2　Why did Orwell live like a poor person at times?

  a　He liked to act and was a gifted actor.

  b　He wanted to save money.

  c　He wanted to research social conditions from personal experience.

  d　He was living away from home and needed lodgings.

  e　During the war everyone lived like a poor person.

Read the following paragraph and add one word from the list to each space so that the paragraph makes sense. There are more words than there are spaces so some will be left out, but each word can only be used once.

brass	combination	consideration	instrument	modern
music	notes	orchestra	ornament	trumpet

-8 The trumpet is a _____ instrument with an extremely long

history. The trumpet is equally at home in an _____, jazz

band or brass band and so it is a deservedly popular _____.

Although it can be traced back to 1500 BC, the _____

trumpet has three or four piston valves which are pushed down, either singularly

or in _____, to create different pitches. Further pitches are

gained by 'embouchure'. This is when the trumpeter controls his or her lips, breath

and facial muscles to extend the range of possible _____.

Select the **ONE** word on the right that has the most **SIMILAR** meaning to the word on the left. Underline the correct answer.

9 pretend   **a** real   **b** genuine   **c** sham   **d** factual   **e** flitter

0 challenge   **a** dare   **b** heroic   **c** brave   **d** action   **e** reaction

1 endless   **a** halt   **b** infinite   **c** insure   **d** direct   **e** indirect

2 intention   **a** aim   **b** reaction   **c** false   **d** reach   **e** motion

Test 30: **Mixed**

Find the three-letter word that is needed to complete each word so that each sentence makes sense. The missing three letters must make a word. Underline the **TWO** answers needed from options **a–e**.

1 The choir sang at the shelte_____ retire_____t home.

    a man   **b** men   **c** red   **d** rod   **e** tar

2 The pool was cool and invigo_____ing after such hot w_____her.

    a ate   **b** eat   **c** oar   **d** rat   **e** rot

The following sentences all have **ONE** word missing. Complete the sentences by selecting a word from options **a–e**.

3 Melt the butter and syrup before stirring in the _____ biscuits.

    a whole   **b** halved   **c** stripped   **d** mashed   **e** crushed

4 The colours of the _____ glass window were beautiful.

    a dirty   **b** smeared   **c** stained   **d** rotten   **e** filthy

Select the **ONE** word on the right that has the most **OPPOSITE** meaning to the word on the left. Underline the correct answer.

5 hectic   **a** still   **b** busy   **c** noisy   **d** rough   **e** level

6 dreary   **a** exactly   **b** raining   **c** bright   **d** dismal   **e** sleepy

Select the **ONE** word on the right that has the most **SIMILAR** meaning to the word on the left. Underline the correct answer.

2

7   eager   **a** early   **b** enthusiastic   **c** easy   **d** energetic   **e** empty

8   fortunate   **a** lucid   **b** luminous   **c** lucky   **d** lush   **e** lurid

Look at the words in the grid and then use them to answer the questions.

8

a wall	**b** perimeter	**c** silky	**d** spear	**e** play
f trill	**g** labour	**h** arrow	**i** pointed	**j** toil
k fair	**l** feed	**m** ascend	**n** sharp	**o** fence
p till	**q** scare	**r** fright	**s** smooth	**t** area
u tile	**v** level	**w** find	**x** shaped	**y** rise

9   Find **TWO** words that are **OPPOSITE** to the word 'rough'.

_____   _____

10   Find **TWO** words that are **OPPOSITE** to the word 'unequal'.

_____   _____

11   Find **TWO** words that are most **SIMILAR** to the word 'work'.

_____   _____

12   Find **TWO** words that are most **SIMILAR** to the word 'climb'.

_____   _____

Total   18

Test 31: **Mixed**

Find the missing three letters that complete these words. The three letters do not have to make a word. The same three letters are used for both words.

1   m_____gement   _____grams

2   ass_____ly   _____arrassment

3   possib_____ty   fac_____ty

Find the missing four letters that need to be added to these words so that the sentence makes sense. The four letters do not have to make a word.

4   The ce_____ity chef was cooking a wonderful meal.

a libr   **b** lebr   **c** lobr   **d** lubr   **e** lebe

5   Akeem checked the date on his cal_____r.

a unda   **b** inda   **c** onda   **d** enda   **e** anda

6   The grey s_____rel hid the acorns and hazelnuts around the forest.

a cwir   **b** cwer   **c** quer   **d** quir   **e** quar

Select the **TWO** odd words out on each line. Select your answers by underlining **TWO** of the options **a–e**.

7   **a** shell   **b** sand   **c** stone   **d** sea   **e** ocean

8   **a** ferry   **b** canoe   **c** van   **d** yacht   **e** bus

9   **a** sharp   **b** pointed   **c** acute   **d** obtuse   **e** fat

Read the following sentences and answer the questions with the most sensible word.

'The cat leapt onto the chair and purred contentedly.'

0 What does the word 'leapt' mean as used in the sentence?

a switched **b** jumped **c** hopped **d** lay **e** rejoiced

1 What does the word 'contentedly' mean as used in the sentence?

a questioningly **b** peacefully **c** miserably **d** sleepily **e** happily

'Jasmine penned a letter to thank her grandmother for her gift.'

2 What does the word 'penned' mean as used in the sentence?

a contained **b** edged **c** posted **d** wrote **e** sent

3 What does the word 'gift' mean as used in the sentence?

a presence **b** present **c** parcel **d** post **e** package

'Elaine gave Alan her discarded burger wrapper before she started the car.'

4 What does the word 'discarded' mean as used in the sentence?

a disliked **b** unwanted **c** retired **d** sad **e** cardboard

5 What does the word 'wrapper' mean as used in the sentence?

a musician **b** packaging **c** singer **d** can **e** plastic

'The spaceman took his first steps in an alien world.'

6 What does the word 'spaceman' mean as used in the sentence?

a cruiser **b** controller **c** captain **d** sailor **e** astronaut

7 What does the word 'alien' mean as used in the sentence?

a extraterrestrial **b** spooky **c** ghostly **d** cosmonaut **e** intelligent

Total 17

Puzzle 1

Anagrams

An anagram is a word with the letters out of order. Unscramble the nature words below. The first one in each list has been done for you.

Trees

ownar	*rowan*
ipen	_____
ako	_____
mel	_____
sha	_____
richb	_____
ebech	_____
owlliw	_____
yohll	_____
camseroy	_____
zealh	_____
peapl	_____
rhycer	_____

Flowers

spyan	*pansy*
sore	_____
uplit	_____
saidy	_____
foldifda	_____
risi	_____
scourc	_____
bullbeel	_____
sockhelenyu	_____
yill	_____
droopswn	_____
mrposier	_____
loveofgx	_____

Puzzle 2

Word Searches

In each of these two word searches, there are 13 words hidden. In the first word search all the words are ways of moving slowly. In the second word search all the words are ways of moving quickly. Find the words and write them on the lines.

```
S  L  O  P  E  S  R  E  M  K
H  W  A  D  D  L  E  Q  E  F
U  M  Y  W  X  I  N  E  C  Z
F  X  A  A  I  N  E  C  X  H
F  K  K  Z  N  K  D  R  W  O
L  S  M  E  C  S  G  A  C  B
E  K  K  B  H  Y  E  W  R  B
L  U  R  C  H  F  N  L  E  L
S  L  O  U  C  H  Y  H  E  E
A  K  T  I  P  T  O  E  P  A
```

_____

_____

_____

_____

_____

_____

_____

_____

_____

_____

_____

_____

```
S  P  E  E  D  T  E  A  R  M
H  K  G  A  L  L  O  P  B  C
Y  S  J  J  P  K  L  H  O  A
D  H  U  R  R  Y  C  I  L  N
A  S  M  X  S  D  Y  J  T  T
S  P  R  I  N  T  Z  P  R  E
H  C  H  O  H  M  C  R  I  R
R  A  C  E  X  E  L  U  P  A
N  D  Y  T  R  O  T  N  Q  P
Q  U  A  B  V  S  G  J  O  G
```

_____

_____

_____

_____

_____

_____

_____

_____

_____

_____

_____

_____

Puzzle 3

Making Hearts

Some words are made up of two shorter words. Match each left-hand half of a heart to a right-hand half to make new words. Write the new words in the hearts below:

Puzzle 4

Homophones

A homophone is a word that sounds the same as another but has a different spelling and meaning. Write a homophone of each word next to it. The first one has been done for you.

brake	_break_	their	_____
hour	_____	tire	_____
dye	_____	dew	_____
reign	_____	aloud	_____
no	_____	rung	_____
buy	_____	sale	_____
sew	_____	seen	_____
yew	_____	made	_____
read	_____	lessen	_____
meet	_____	feint	_____
led	_____	floor	_____
steel	_____	find	_____
reel	_____	stair	_____

Puzzle 5

What a Muddle!

These words have all been muddled up. Put each one into the correct list.

tempting	minuscule	enormous	massive	scrumptious
delicious	huge	succulent	gigantic	disgusting
appetizing	revolting	sickly	bitter	unpalatable
tiny	little	vast	minute	miniature

Big _____ _____ _____

_____ _____

Small _____ _____ _____

_____ _____

Tasty _____ _____ _____

_____ _____

Inedible _____ _____ _____

_____ _____

Puzzle 6

Make a List

Each list of words has **ONE** word that does not fit. Find the odd words out and put them into List 6. All of the remaining words in each list have a similar meaning.

List 1	List 2	List 3
neat	fall	climb
pale	drop	lift
presentable	descend	ascend
tidy	white	rise
immaculate	plunge	wan
orderly	plummet	soar

List 4	List 5	List 6
foam	ashen	_____
froth	bury	_____
lather	cover	_____
bubbles	hide	_____
spray	conceal	_____
bleached	disguise	

Puzzle 7

Find the opposite of each clue to complete the crossword.

Across

3	sister (7)	**5**	boiling (8)
8	cramped (8)	**10**	victim (5)
6	closed (6)	**12**	woman (3)

Across

- **3** sister (7)
- **8** cramped (8)
- **5** boiling (8)
- **10** victim (5)
- **6** closed (6)
- **12** woman (3)

Down

- **1** father (6)
- **7** quiet (5)
- **2** enemy (6)
- **9** dirty (5)
- **4** slow (5)
- **11** high (3)

Puzzle 8

Alphabet Challenge

Here is a list of categories. Find one word for each category that begins with the letters in the grid above. The first one has been completed as an example. If you manage this, why not try using some other letters of the alphabet?

CATEGORIES	A	B	C
Animal	antelope		
Boy's name	Ahmed		
Food item	apricot		
Girl's name	Abigail		
Plant	aspen tree		
Sport/hobby	archery		

CATEGORIES	F	G	H
Animal			
Boy's name			
Food item			
Girl's name			
Plant			
Sport/hobby			

CATEGORIES	K	L	M
Animal			
Boy's name			
Food item			
Girl's name			
Plant			
Sport/hobby			

Progress chart

How did you do? Fill in your score below and shade in the corresponding boxes to compare your progress across the different tests.

| | 50% | 100% | 50% | 1 |

Test 1, p2 Score: _____ /13

Test 2, p4 Score: _____ /15

Test 3, p6 Score: _____ /18

Test 4, p8 Score: _____ /13

Test 5, p10 Score: _____ /17

Test 6, p12 Score: _____ /15

Test 7, p14 Score: _____ /20

Test 8, p16 Score: _____ /20

Test 9, p18 Score: _____ /7

Test 10, p20 Score: _____ /17

Test 11, p22 Score: _____ /22

Test 12, p24 Score: _____ /17

Test 13, p26 Score: _____ /9

Test 14, p28 Score: _____ /20

Test 15, p30 Score: _____ /18

Test 16, p32 Score: _____ /17

Test 17, p34 Score: _____ /14

Test 18, p36 Score: _____ /13

Test 19, p46 Score: _____ /19

Test 20, p48 Score: _____ /21

Test 21, p50 Score: _____ /21

Test 22, p52 Score: _____ /12

Test 23, p54 Score: _____ /20

Test 24, p56 Score: _____ /19

Test 25, p58 Score: _____ /19

Test 26, p60 Score: _____ /12

Test 27, p62 Score: _____ /13

Test 28 p64 Score: _____ /17

Test 29, p66 Score: _____ /13

Test 30, p68 Score: _____ /18

Test 31, p70 Score: _____ /17